11/19

Handprint Art

Handprint Animals

By
Henu Mehtani

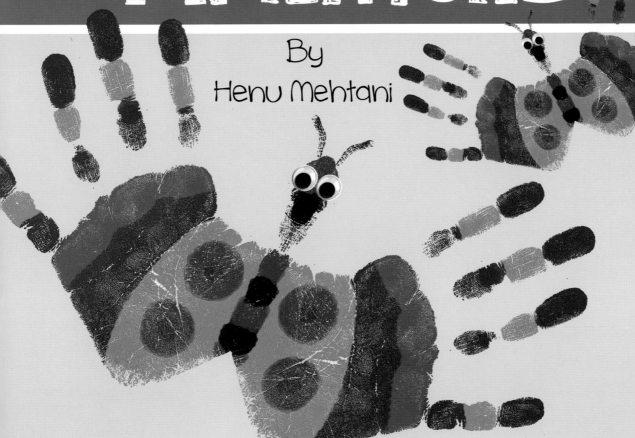

 Crabtree Publishing Company
www.crabtreebooks.com

Crabtree Publishing Company

www.crabtreebooks.com
1-800-387-7650

616 Welland Ave.
St. Catharines, ON
L2M 5V6

PMB 59051, 350 Fifth Ave.
59th Floor,
New York, NY 10118

Published in 2017 by CRABTREE PUBLISHING COMPANY.

Author: Henu Mehtani

Illustrator: Henu Mehtani

Editorial director: Felicia Law

Project Coordinator: , Kathy Middleton

Editors: Saranne Taylor, Petrice Custance

Proofreader: Wendy Scavuzzo

Prepress technician: Tammy McGarr

Print coordinator: Katherine Berti

Art and Illustrations: Copyright © 2015
Henu Studio Pvt. Ltd.
All rights reserved
www.henustudio.com

Edition copyright © 2015 BrambleKids Ltd

Printed in Hong Kong/012017/BK20161024

Library and Archives Canada Cataloguing in Publication

Mehtani, Henu, author
        Handprint animals / Henu Mehtani.

(Handprint art)
ISBN 978-0-7787-3108-5 (hardback).--
ISBN 978-0-7787-3112-2 (paperback)

        1. Finger painting--Juvenile literature. 2. Animals in art--Juvenile literature. 3. Painting--Technique--Juvenile literature. 4. Handicraft for children--Juvenile literature. I. Title.

ND2490.M44 2016   j751.4'9   C2016-906645-2

Library of Congress Cataloging-in Publication Data

Names: Mehtani, Henu, author.
Title: Handprint animals / Henu Mehtani.
Description: New York, New York : Crabtree Publishing, [2017] |
    Series: Handprint art | Audience: Age 5-8. | Audience: K to grade 3. |
    Includes index.
Identifiers: LCCN 2016046754|
    ISBN 9780778731085 (hardcover : alk. paper) |
    ISBN 9780778731122 (pbk. : alk. paper)
Subjects: LCSH: Art--Technique--Juvenile literature. | Animals in
    art--Juvenile literature. | Fingerprints in art--Juvenile literature.
Classification: LCC N7433 .M353 2017 | DDC 700/.462--dc23
LC record available at https://lccn.loc.gov/2016046754

Contents

You will need

- Drawing paper or a sketch book
- Tempera paints. The more colors the better!
- Paintbrushes. Try different sizes, such as a round brush, a thin brush, and a flat brush.
- Apron and cloths for keeping clean
- Your own hands!

Tips

- Work on the background of your artwork before you make your handprint animals. You can either copy the backgrounds from this book, or you can design your own!
- Remember to allow the paint to dry between layers. Be sure to wash your hands before switching to a new color.

Experiment

- Try using different colors than the colors listed in the book. Be creative!
- Once you have practiced on paper, you can try to make pictures and designs on a T-shirt or pillow case. Just use fabric paints instead!

Kingfisher

What to do

- Paint your left hand blue and pink as shown on this kingfisher.

- Print your hand on the paper with closed fingers.

- To make the face, paint your thumb blue and pink as shown on this kingfisher. Print your thumb.

- Use a thin brush to paint the **beak**, **crest**, and feet.

- Paint on googly eyes.

Walrus

What to do

- Paint your left hand brown. Print your hand on the paper with your thumb stretched out.

- Print your full thumb to make the second front flipper.

- Use different shades of brown to make the **muzzle** and the mouth.

- Use a fine brush to paint the nose, whiskers, eyebrows, and **tusks**.

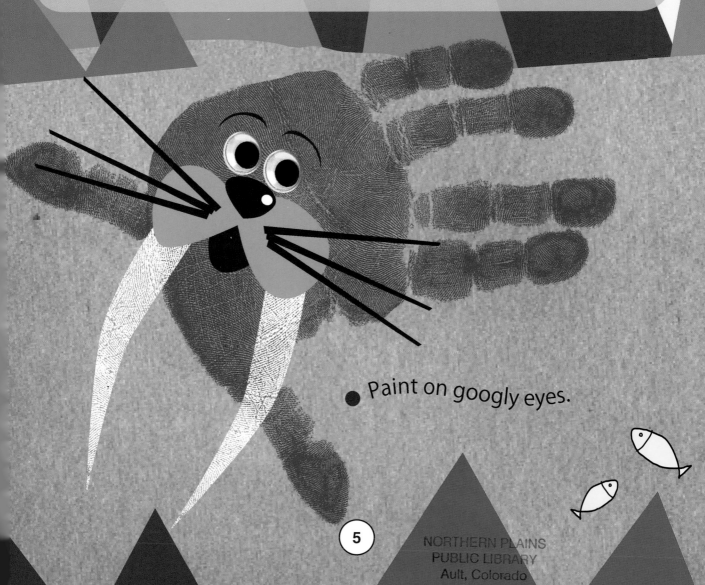

- Paint on googly eyes.

Alligator

What to do

- Paint your right hand green. Print it on the paper with your fingers closed. This makes the body.

- Paint your left hand green. Print it on the paper facing the other way to make the head. Keep your fingers apart in the middle to make the mouth.

- Paint a darker green on your fingertips. Make the scales along the alligator's back and spots on its body.

- Use a flat brush to paint the front leg.

- Use a thin brush to paint the teeth, tongue, **nostrils**, and claws.

- Paint on googly eyes.

Flamingos

What to do

- Paint your left hand pink. Print it on the paper with your thumb stretched out.

- Using fingerprints, make the neck and face.

- Paint on googly eyes.

- Use a thin brush to paint the beak, legs, and feet.

- Now do the same with your right hand. Make a pair of flamingos!

Butterflies

What to do

- Paint a pattern of your choice on both of your hands.

- Print them on the paper, keeping your thumbs away from the paper.

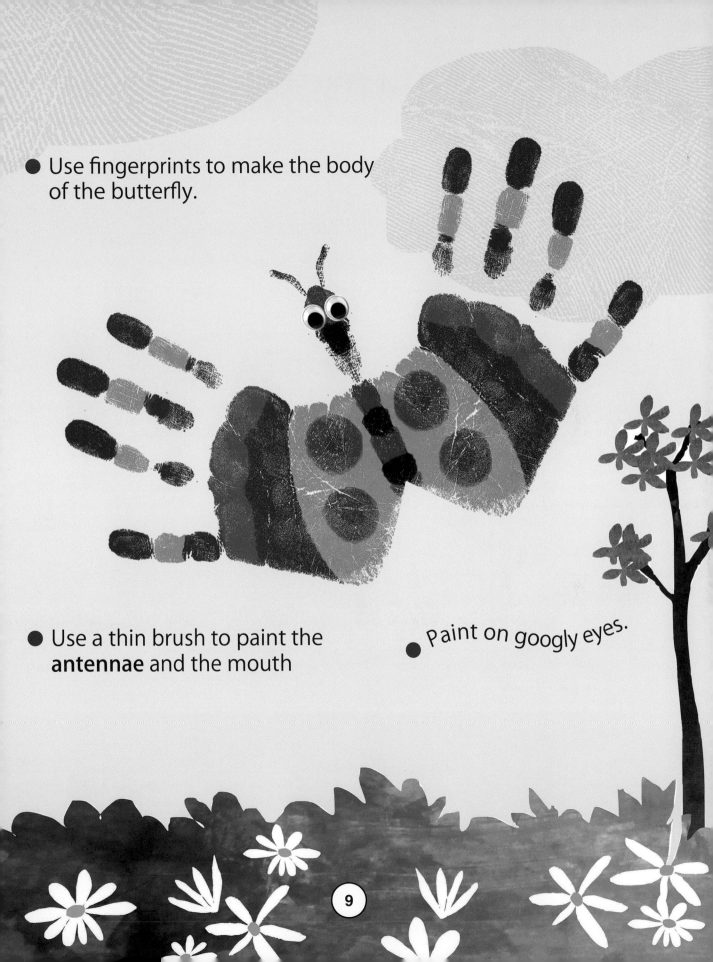

● Use fingerprints to make the body of the butterfly.

● Use a thin brush to paint the **antennae** and the mouth

● Paint on googly eyes.

Camels

What to do

- Paint your hand brown. Print it upside down with your thumb sticking out to make the body of the camel.

- Use half a fingerprint to make the neck. Use a thumbprint to make the face.

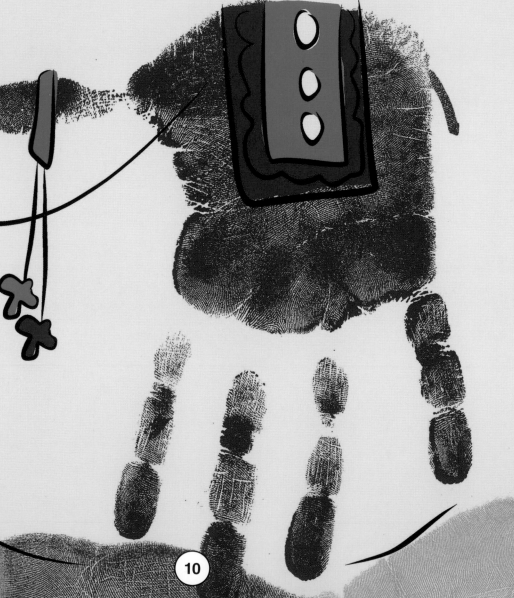

- Use a thin brush to paint the ears, tail, and **reins**.

- Decorate the camel with a colorful **saddle**.

- Paint on googly eyes.

Yak

What to do

- Paint both your hands brown. Print them upside down next to each other.

- Paint your fingers a darker brown. Print them on the paper to make the yak's body hair and **hooves**.

- Use a thin brush to paint the face, horns, muzzle, nostrils, and ears.

- Paint on googly eyes.

12

Deer

What to do

- Paint your right hand light brown. Print it upside down on the paper to make the deer's body.

- Use your thumbprint to make the face.

- Paint the tips of your fingers with black. Make spots on its body.

- Use a thin brush to paint on the tail and **antlers**.

- Paint on googly eyes.

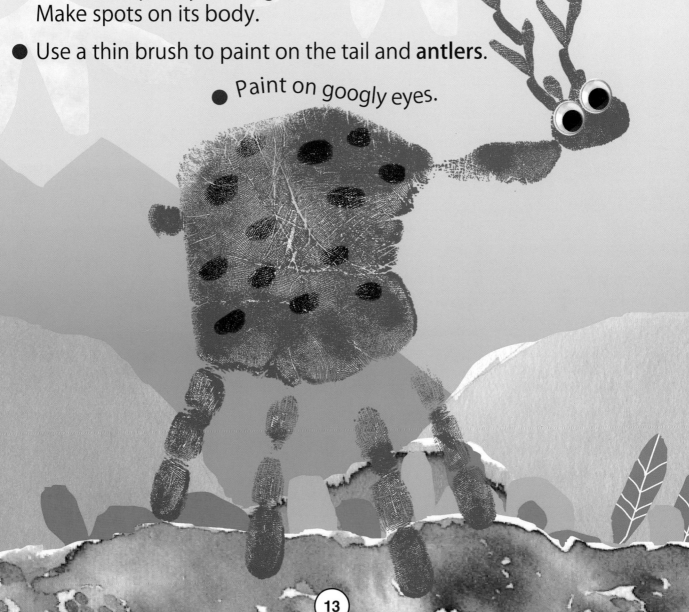

Elephants

What to do

- Mix blue and gray paint together and paint your hand.

- Print it upside down with your fingers stretched out to make the body and trunk.

- Use a thin brush to paint on the tusks, ears, tail, and hooves.

- Paint on googly eyes.

Giraffe

What to do

- Paint your left hand orange. Print it upside down with your fingers stretched out.

- Use fingerprints to make the neck.

- Paint the tips of your fingers brown to make the dark spots on the giraffe's body, tail, and hooves.

- Use a thin brush to make the ears, **horns**, nostrils, and the mouth.

- Paint on googly eyes.

15

Paint on googly eyes.

16

Hen

What to do

- Paint your right hand white. Print it on the paper with your thumb stretched out.

- Paint your fingerprints light orange. Use them to make the wing feathers.

- Use your thumbprint to make the egg.

- Use a thin brush to paint the beak, **comb**, and **wattle**.

- Paint on googly eyes.

Quail

What to do

- Paint your left hand with gray, blue, and brown as shown on this quail. Print your hand on the paper.

- Make the face with a thumbprint.

- Use a thin brush to, paint the beak, feet, and **plume**.

Jaguar

● Paint on googly eyes.

What to do

● Paint your hand deep yellow. Print it on the paper with your fingers spread out for the legs.

● Complete the long tail using two fingerprints.

● Use a fine brush to paint the face, spots, and claws.

18

Monkey

What to do

- Mix deep yellow and brown paints and paint your hand.

- Print it on the paper with your fingers spread out to make the body and legs of the monkey.

- Use a fine brush to paint the mouth, ears, tail, and the fingered hands and feet.

- Paint on googly eyes.

Ladybug

What to do

- Paint both your hands with red paint.

- Print them close together keeping your thumbs away from the paper.

- Use your fingertips to paint black spots on the body.

- Use a fine brush to paint the face, antennae, and legs.

- Paint on googly eyes.

Caterpillar

What to do

● Paint your left hand green and print it on the paper. Wash your hand and paint it yellow. Print it next to the green print. Repeat two more times to make the body.

● Use a round brush to paint the face. Use fingerprints to make the antennae. Use a fine brush to paint the mouth, tongue, and teeth.

● Paint your fingertips orange and make dots on the caterpillar's body.

● Paint on googly eyes.

Narwhal

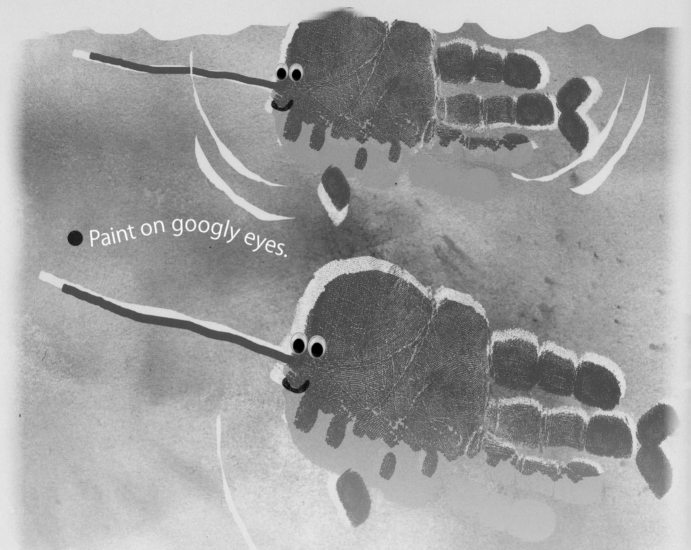

● Paint on googly eyes.

What to do

● Paint your left hand with white, dark blue, and light blue paint as shown above. Make a print with your fingers closed.

● Use fingerprints to make the tail **fins** and a fin underneath the body.

● Use a fine brush to paint the mouth and the long tusk.

X-ray fish

What to do

- Paint your hand black. Print it on the paper with your fingers spread out.

- Using white paint and a flat brush, paint the skeleton of the fish.

- Paint on googly eyes.

Penguin

Paint on googly eyes.

What to do

- Paint your left hand black with a long white oval in the center that goes from the middle of your hand halfway down your fingers. Print it upside down with your thumb and little finger stickng out to make wings.

- Paint on the orange beak and feet with a fine brush.

24

Polar bear

What to do

- Paint your hand white and print it upside down. Make the tail with a white thumbprint.

- Use a round brush to paint the face.

- Paint on googly eyes.

- With black, gray, and brown paints, use your fingertips to make the muzzle, nose, and ears. Paint the mouth with a fine brush.

Paint on googly eyes.

Owl

What to do

- Paint your hand with different shades of gray and brown. Print upside down on the paper with your fingers together.

- Use fingerprints to make the white spots on the chest.

- Use a fine brush to paint the beak, ears, and **talons**.

Fox

What to do

- Paint your right hand. Print it upside down with your thumb stretched out.

- Use fingerprints to make the feet and to make the tail thicker.

- Use a fine brush to paint the face, nose, ears, and teeth.

- Paint on googly eyes.

Sheep

What to do

● Paint your hand white. Print it upside down on the paper with your fingers spread out to make the legs.

● Use a thumbprint to make the head.

● Use gray fingerprints to make the hooves.

● Use a fine brush to paint the mouth, ears, and tail.

● Paint on googly eyes.

Horse

● Paint on googly eyes.

What to do

● Paint your hand brown.
Print it upside down on
the paper with your fingers
spread out.

● Use fingerprints to
make the tail.

● Using dark brown paint on
your fingertips, make the tail
ends, hooves, and muzzle.

● Paint your fingertips with
deep yellow and use them
to make the **mane**.

● Use a fine brush to paint the
nostrils and ears.

Zebra

What to do

- Paint your hand white. Print it upside down on the paper with your fingers spread out.

- Use your fingertips to make the hooves and muzzle.

- Use a fine brush. Paint the stripes, mane, ears, and tail.

- Paint on googly eyes.

30

Vultures

What to do

- Paint your hand black and print it on the paper.

- Use a thumbprint to make the head and neck.

- Use a fine brush to paint the neck ruffles, white feathers, beak, eyebrows, and claws.

- Paint on googly eyes.

Glossary

antennae Threadlike feelers on the head of an insect

antlers Bony structures that grow from the head of a deer or a similar animal

beak A hard pointed part that covers a bird's mouth

comb A soft fleshy part on the head of some birds

crest A showy growth, such as feathers, on the head of an animal

fins Thin parts on the body of a water animal that are used to move or guide the body through the water

hooves Hard coverings on the feet of some animals

horns Hard pointed parts that grow on the head of some animals

mane Hair that grows from the neck of some animals

muzzle The nose and mouth area of some animals

nostrils The two openings of a nose

plume A large or showy feather on a bird

reins The straps attached to a device that is placed on an animal and used to control or guide it

saddle A seat for the rider of an animal

talons Sharp claws on the feet of some birds

tusks Large teeth that stick out of the mouth of some animals

wattle A fleshy flap of skin that hangs from the neck of some birds

Learning more

Books

Corfee, Stephanie. *Paint Lab for Kids: 52 Creative Adventures in Painting and Mixed Media for Budding Artists of All Ages.* Quarry Books, 2015.

Levy, Barbara Soloff. *How to Draw Animals.* Dover Publications, 2008.

Websites

Visit this site for tons of handprint craft ideas:
www.dltk-kids.com/type/handprint.htm

Check out this fun online painting machine:
**www.nga.gov/content/ngaweb/
education/kids/kids-brushster.html**